60 DAY REBUILD

Copyright © Gerritt Bake

Firefly & Wisp Books 2019

All rights reserved. Except for use in any review, the reproduction or use of this work in whole or in part in any form by any electronic, mechanical or other means, now know or hereafter invented, including xerography, photocopying and recording, or in any information storage or retrieval system is forbidden without the permission of Firefly and Wisp Publishing and Gerritt Bake Tactical Businessman™.

Warning: the unauthorized reproduction or distribution of this copyrighted work is illegal. Criminal copyright infringement, including infringement without monetary gain is investigated by the FBI and is punishable by up to 5 years in prison and a fine of $250,000. All rights reserved. No part of this book may be reproduced or transmitted in any form without written permission from the publisher, except by a reviewer who may quote brief passages for review purposes.

My brother,

Could we stop pretending for a minute?

I don't know you. But I do.

You, like me, are struggling in life.

It could be with your body, your sense of purpose, your relationship with your wife, your business…or all of the above.

But frankly, it doesn't matter. Neither does where or how you grew up. Or your current situation.

The truth is simple: Your life isn't working the way you want it to.

That's it. No sugar coat. No complex explanation.

You simply want more.

And trying to figure it out on your own hasn't worked for you. Just like it didn't for me.

That's why I created this program. This is the foundational blueprint I followed to turn my life around.

I'm here to tell you that it is possible to have it all.

A body that's in shape and full of energy.

A relationship that's on fire and filled with passion.

A business that thrives and fills the coffers with passion and profit.

But I can't create this life for you. No one can.

Except for you.

It's time to wake up.

It's time to take action.

It's time to quit playing on the sidelines of your own life.

There is only one thing left to do.

Go ALL IN on you.

That's it.

Time to get after it,

Gerritt Bake

-Founder, The Tactical Businessman

-Creator, The Tactical Businessman 60 Day Rebuild

WEEK ONE - FOUNDATION
DAY 1 MONDAY

"Be yourself. Everyone else is taken." - Oscar Wilde

WHO ARE YOU

THE REASON YOU ARE HERE IS BECAUSE YOU WANT MORE. Whatever is going on in your life right now isn't working the way you want it to. You are experiencing pain and discomfort. And you want more.

The Process For Getting More:

1. You must be experiencing Pain.
2. You must have a DESIRE to relieve that Pain.
3. You must have a willingness to go ALL IN on yourself and stop hiding.

How This System Works: Leverage the workbook, audio, and video to deliver a 3-dimensional experience. This allows you to liberate yourself to finally achieve the success in both your personal and professional life that you've always dreamed of.

RULES:

1. Only Relevant Conversation - No business promotion
2. Strictly Private Confidentiality - No sharing of any information in this group whatsoever, with family members, friends or the public.
3. About Groups - Do not create any separate groups, otherwise you will get booted.
4. Respect your Coaches at all times.

THE 5 STANDARDS:

1. Trust The Process - Follow the plan we outline, even when it gets hard or when you don't understand it.
2. Details Matter - What we layout requires a level of focus. If you plan to do this half-assed, you may as well not do it. Focus on the details.
3. Be Here Now - Don't waste time here... it's designed for you to gain value from and engage with brothers, not as another tool of sedation. When you're here. You're here. If you're using this as just another tool for sedation...then get out.
4. Don't Ever Quit - You may want to quit. You're going to feel pressure. When you get off the bandwagon, it's okay. Get back on. Brush yourself off and get back in the game.
5. Take Care Of Your Brothers: In order to make it through this training and your life, you can no longer survive playing solo.

ASSIGNMENT

1. Upload A Profile Picture: Just a picture of your face, most recent, selfie, no sunglasses or hats, no hiding

2. Create "The Why" Album: Upload family pictures. Add the name of your Wife/Significant Other and Kids in the comment section.

3. Audio - Drop a One minute or less audio in your squad chat group answering the following questions: Who are you? Name? What do you do? Where are you from? Married not married? Why are you here?

WEEK ONE - FOUNDATION
DAY 2 TUESDAY

"Half a truth is often a great lie." - Benjamin Franklin

LIES

HOW DID YOU GET HERE?

1. The path we took to get here may be different. Some of you have marriages that are falling apart. Some of you: businesses that are crumbling. Some of you have failing health. It doesn't matter if it's one of these or a combination. What got you to this point was the lies you told yourself. And the crazy part is, regardless of our situation, the lies we tell ourselves are the same.
2. The lies could have started weeks or months ago. A few years or decades. It doesn't matter where or when they started. They put you in this place where you feel overwhelmed. Unhappy. Discontent. Hatred. Anger. Frustration. Sad.
3. These lies we have told created our current situation. Our current reality.

THE TWO TYPES OF LIES:

1. <u>Lies of Commission</u>: Overt lies where we mingle a piece of the truth with a whole lot of lies. Example: Small-I didn't eat that ice cream (when you know you did) Large-I wasn't looking at porn (when you know you were).
2. <u>Lies of Omission</u>: Lies we purposely tell ourselves. Small-I can still run a 6-minute mile. Large-I can't tell my wife I lost a ton of money because she won't love me anymore.

EXTERNAL AND INTERNAL LIES:

1. <u>External</u>: Lies we tell others-I'm better than I really am (as long as I can tell stories they will like me)

2. <u>Internal</u>: Lies we tell ourselves-I'm not good enough (if I tell you how I'm thinking or feeling, you'll reject me)

WHERE THAT HAS PUT YOU TODAY? It's literally killing you. Causing you to run and hide from the truth. Through whatever means necessary. Hiding your porn addiction in the bathroom. Staying out late drinking with "friends". Popping pills. Staying up late playing video games. Drowning the family out with social media. Working 20 hours a day not making more money but just trying to stay busy.

ASSIGNMENT

Answer the following questions:

1. What is the biggest lie you are telling yourself today?

_____
_____
_____
_____
_____
_____
_____

2. What is the biggest lie you are telling others today?

_____
_____
_____
_____
_____
_____
_____

WEEK ONE - FOUNDATION
DAY 3 WEDNESDAY

"Labels put people in boxes, and those boxes are shaped like coffins." - Chirlane McCray

---

THE LABELS

WHAT ARE THEY? A word or phrase indicating that what follows belongs in a particular category or classification (Dictionary.com) In other words, most labels put you in a box. They restrict your movement, your freedom. Like your own coffin.

WHERE DO THEY COME FROM? As America began to define itself as a nation, it also had to redefine its individuals. Where a man once lived and worked with his family, by the sweat of his brow, he was now expected to leave that family to work in a factory in exchange for a "pension", healthcare, and other guarantees. What did this do? It caused the eventual disconnect and disintegration of the family.

1. <u>External Labels</u> (society)
   What they tell us we are through religion, culture, socioeconomic, advertising
2. <u>Internal Labels</u> (ourselves)
   What we believe ourselves to be (fat, skinny, smart, dumb, not good enough, unable to speak clearly)

HOW DO THEY DETERMINE THE REALITY WITHIN WHICH WE LIVE? We internalize this and say, "This is who I am." I am a soldier therefore I have no feelings and emotions and I just want to kill the bad guy. I am a businessman therefore I don't have time to be a good husband or father. Raising my kids is my wife's responsibility.

THE TRUTH IS... WE DON'T EVEN KNOW WHAT IT

MEANS TO BE A **MAN** ANYMORE.

ASSIGNMENT

Answer the questions:

1. What are the 3 biggest labels are you carrying today?

   _____
   _____
   _____
   _____
   _____
   _____

2. Who gave them to you?

   _____
   _____
   _____
   _____
   _____
   _____

3. Write out the 3 labels and who put them on you, take a picture in front of the mirror with the 3 labels, and post it in the group. Then, drop a one-minute audio talking about what you learned in your squad chat group.

WEEK ONE - FOUNDATION
DAY 4 THURSDAY

"If you tell the truth, you don't have to remember anything." - Mark Twain

---

THE TRUTH

WHAT IS THE DEFINITION OF TRUTH? You have been taught to lie. Since you were a child. What your friends thought was acceptable. What your family tolerated. Taught to suppress your feelings and insecurities. Because it's not cool. It's not socially acceptable. And you're still playing that game.

WHAT'S THE PRICE TO PAY? There is always a price to pay. You're body takes a toll (unhealthy, out of shape, tired, stressed), your relationship takes a hit (lack of trust and sex), your business grinds to a halt (you don't know how to fix the problem, you run out of money, you are angry and bitter and scare everyone, including clients and employees, away)

YOU CREATED THE RULES YOU'RE PLAYING BY. These labels, some of which stretch into your childhood, created the life you live by. They were your "code". And the results you are experiencing are based solely on these. You've been telling yourself these lies for so long it's hard to uncover where lies end and truth begins.

ASSIGNMENT

What has been the true cost of you hiding behind these labels and not telling yourself the truth about your current situation?

WEEK ONE - FOUNDATION
DAY 5 FRIDAY

"Two roads diverged in a wood, and I - I took the one less traveled by, and that has made all the difference." - Robert Frost

---

THE DARK

WATCH THE VIDEO FIRST

IT'S TIME TO FACE THE TRUTH-who you really are and what you really want. Fear of the dark is something that has been instilled in us since we were young. Where is truth hiding? In the dark. The darkness has followed us since our childhood. We have become prisoners to our own darkness...our own truth.

The idea that we ARE more...that we are worth more, is one that we chase after. But something happened.

BUT WE GAVE UP TRYING. Years ago. We feel stuck. Surrounded by our own darkness. Can't see anything. Unable to stand and find a path out because our labels and our lies have kept us prisoner here. These lies keep us confined; to what we eat, how we act, what we do.

We keep telling ourselves that we are ok in this place. Another lie added to the wall. But you can't run from it anymore.

HOW DO YOU OVERCOME THIS DARKNESS? This fear of the truth? By finally facing it. Telling yourself the truth of what is working and what is not working for you right now.

I can never forget the excruciating pain I felt surrounded in my own darkness. Helpless. Alone. Afraid. The pain of being disconnected from my wife and children. The story that I was doing everything in my power to be there for them. To love

them. A story that everything was ok and I was happy. And that it wasn't affecting my career. My ability to focus and produce. Nobody knew. I would hide the pain. No one gets me anyway. I hid behind the labels. Producer. Man. Elite.

And all this did was force me to spend more time at work than at home trying to repair everything I had broken. How was it possible that I would believe that for 15 years? Because I wasn't willing to sit in the dark and feel the pain. My own pain. The pain I inflicted on others.
I had become elite at telling myself the story that I was ok. That there wasn't anything wrong with me. And that my family loved me.

IT'S TIME TO FACE THE DARKNESS. This task will not be easy. You must face the reality that you've been hiding from. The truth in your life.

ASSIGNMENT

1. Find a dark room or dark night.

2. Sit in the dark for 5 minutes and think about the pain you are feeling right now in your life in the following areas...

   Where are you today? What's working? But more importantly...what's not?

   Physically? Emotionally? Relationship? Financially?

   What is it like not to have the life you want? To feel alone?

   This is the doorway to liberation. You weren't meant to be here. In the dark. Alone. But the only way to find the light... is to hunt it in the night.

3. When you have completed your 5 minutes, find a dark place somewhere and record a two-minute video and post in your squad chat group where you answer the following question:

   Describe your current darkness you see and feel in your life right now.

WEEK TWO - UNREALITY
DAY 1 MONDAY

*"Three things cannot be long hidden.
The sun, the moon, and the truth."* - Buddha

THE CODE

WHAT IS THE TRUTH? Reality. Peace. Exactly where you're at right now. Not based on some feeling or emotion, but the facts.

But most of us have grown accustomed to our own skewed version of the truth. Where do the lies end...and the truth start? After a while, you're so deep in your lies that you can't even remember anymore. The crazy part? You don't have to remember the truth, because there is only one version of it.

HOW TRUTHFUL ARE YOU WITH YOURSELF? So where are you at right now? What does this little world you've built look like? If you're struggling to answer that...you're not alone.

HOW TRUTHFUL ARE YOU WITH OTHERS? Being honest with yourself is scary enough...but being honest with others? Does your wife know your biggest fears? Do your children know your failures? Do your employees or business partners know the truth about the health of your business or your struggles in it?

The feelings that surround the truth (both positive and negative), reinforce the lies. Society teaches us that telling the truth will make us "feel" a certain way. They try and dissuade us from it. All the ads you see are based on lies and manipulation. A car won't make you happy. A shake won't make you skinny. And a sexy piece of lingerie won't fix your marriage.

YOU'RE TOLD IF YOU LIE TO YOURSELF, THEN YOU'LL BE HAPPY. If you tell the truth...you'll feel guilt and shame. So where would you rather be?

ASSIGNMENT

Answer the following questions:

1. What does it mean to you to tell the truth?

___

2. When is the last time you told the whole truth?

___

3. Drop a one-minute audio in your squad chat group sharing your answers.

WEEK TWO - UNREALITY
DAY 2 TUESDAY

"What screws us up most in life is the picture in our head of how it is supposed to be." - Jeremy Bins

EXPECTATIONS

THE IMPOSSIBLE TARGET

The movie "Wanted" with Angelina Jolie is all about bending reality. A group of vigilantes who have the ability to curve bullets. Hitting the "Impossible Target" behind or through someone. But we all know it was a fantasy. A lie.

Remember Enron? The multibillion-dollar poster child of Wall Street. Unrealistic returns. A beautiful yet flawed painting of reality. But it was all a lie. And eventually, the truth came out. December 2008 was the start of Bernie Madoff's downfall. For years he had bilked investors to the tune of almost $65 billion dollars. The largest Ponzi scheme in history. And the lie had finally caught up with him. Now he is spending the rest of his life in prison.

CHASING THE IMPOSSIBLE GAME

Where do unrealistic expectations lead you? To a place of never being satisfied. You're constantly running and hiding or constantly wanting more. There is never enough satisfaction. So you keep going. How long can you keep it up? Eventually you wear yourself out. Too tired to keep up the facade. Too worn out to keep lying. You WANT to be caught. Because then you don't have to tell the lie anymore.

ASSIGNMENT

Answer the following questions:

1. What is one unrealistic expectation you have set for yourself based on a lie you continue to tell?

___

2. How does it make you feel?

___

WEEK TWO - UNREALITY
DAY 3 WEDNESDAY

"None knows the weight of another's burden." - George Herbert

---

THE BURDEN

THE WEIGHT OF THE WORLD ON YOUR SHOULDERS IS HEAVY. And it doesn't get any lighter. Especially if you're filling your backpack with rocks. The rocks of lies. Of unrealistic expectations. It just gets heavier and heavier.

What does it cause you to do? Eventually, no matter how "strong" you are, the burden starts to wear you down. You are constantly stopping. Taking breaks. Your mind starts to wear out. And your body soon follows. Pretty soon you become a shell of yourself. Alone. Thrown on the side of the road. Passed over and passed by. By those who used to be close to you. Your own family and friends.

YOU LOSE FOCUS ON WHAT MATTERS TO YOU because it's no longer around. Your wife becomes a roommate. Your kids? You're their ATM. Your business starts to struggle. And eventually you would rather burn it to the ground than to continue.

WHAT'S THE COST THAT THE EMOTIONAL AND FINANCIAL LIES CARRY?

The divorce rate amongst businessmen is 10% higher than the rest of the population.

The rate of drug addiction is 20% higher.

The suicide rate has jumped 30% since 1999.

Depression runs rampant.

And time runs out.

ASSIGNMENT

Answer the following questions:

1. Based on the biggest lie you told someone else (Week One Day 2), what has been the cost for carrying on with that lie?

___

2. What would it feel like to be free from that burden?

___

3. Drop a one-minute audio in your squad chat group sharing your answers.

WEEK TWO - UNREALITY
DAY 4 THURSDAY

"A wise man proportions his belief to the evidence."- David Hume

BELIEFS

SOMETIMES, AS YOU'RE RUSHING THROUGH LIFE, YOU CATCH A GLIMPSE OF YOURSELF IN THE MIRROR. You stop dead in your tracks. "Who am I? Who have I become?" The person you see is not who you thought you were. You see a man that is struggling. Alone. Feeling broken. Afraid. Depressed.

THE DEFINITION OF INSANITY IS DOING THE SAME THING OVER AND OVER AGAIN EXPECTING DIFFERENT RESULTS. Why are you doing what you are if it doesn't bring you happiness? Most of us don't know the answer to that. And we don't know where to look. So we just keep doing what we know how to do. Struggle. Hustle. Grind. Lie.

THERE IS A SAYING THAT HAS BEEN USED FOR THOUSANDS OF YEARS. The straw that broke the camel's back. The breaking point. It wasn't the weight of all the straw that broke the back. It was the last straw. And so it is in your life. We finally get to the point where it breaks us.

ASSIGNMENT

Answer the following questions:

1. How have the lies you've told yourself influenced who you believe yourself to be?

   _____
   _____
   _____
   _____
   _____
   _____
   _____
   _____
   _____

2. How much pressure do you feel from these false beliefs?

   _____
   _____
   _____
   _____
   _____
   _____
   _____
   _____

WEEK TWO - UNREALITY
DAY 5 FRIDAY

"The underbelly of the human psyche, what is often referred to as our dark side, is the origin of every act of self-sabotage. Birthed out of shame, fear, and denial, it misdirects our good intentions and drives us to unthinkable acts of self-destruction and not-so-unbelievable acts of self-sabotage." - Debbie Ford

---

CYCLE OF SELF SABOTAGE

WHAT IS THE CYCLE OF SELF SABOTAGE? It has 6 phases

1. The Quiet Little Lie
2. Suppression
3. Isolation
4. Sedation
5. Feeling Alone
6. Unworthiness

HOW YOU FIND YOURSELF STUCK IN IT? Your frustration and confusion with what's happening or not happening in your life starts this cycle. You tell yourself there has to be something wrong...or "I'm broken". And once you start that cycle, it's hard to stop.

WHAT IS IT COSTING YOU? All these feelings eventually lead you to a place where you don't even feel worthy of your life anymore. So you consciously begin to tear your marriage apart. To burn your business to the ground. To lash out in anger and pain. Till you eventually end up alone and broken.

HOW DO YOU BREAK FREE?

Your current system of dealing with the frustration and confusion of life isn't working. It's got you caught up in this cycle. There is a way to break free, though. It begins with acknowledging that you are the source of all your problems...but also the source of all of your solutions. Then, being empowered, you break free of the old operating system you had. And you create a new one. A new one centered around one concept: Having It All.

ASSIGNMENT

WATCH THE VIDEO FIRST

1. Complete the activity titled "Cycle of Self Sabotage" on the next page by defining one specific cycle in your life.

2. Identify the financial and emotional costs associated with this cycle.

_____
_____
_____
_____
_____
_____
_____
_____
_____

3. When you have completed the assignment, record a one-minute video inside you squad group where you talk about your cycle and the financial and emotional costs you identified.

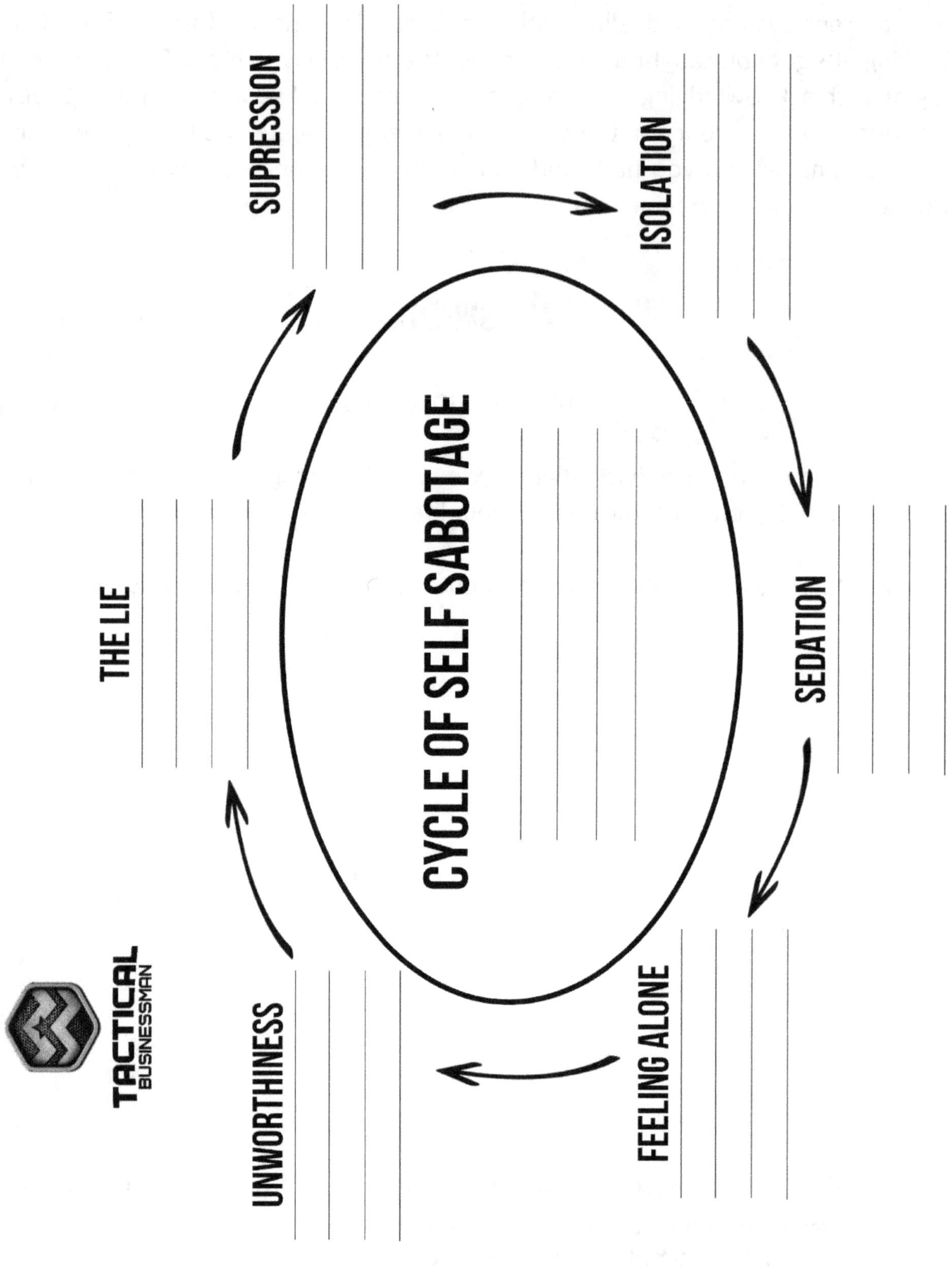
CYCLE OF SELF SABOTAGE
THE LIE
SUPRESSION
ISOLATION
SEDATION
FEELING ALONE
UNWORTHINESS
TACTICAL BUSINESSMAN

(NOTES)

WEEK THREE - LIBERATION
DAY 1 MONDAY

"The trouble with lying and deceiving is that their efficiency depends entirely upon a clear notion of the truth that the liar and deceiver wishes to hide." - Hannah Arendt

---

MAN IN THE MIRROR

YOU CAN'T FAKE IT TILL YOU MAKE IT IN LIFE. The reason you don't have the relationship or the business or the body you want is simple. You've been told since you were young to "fake it till you make it". And you've been so busy faking it that the only thing you worry about any more is keeping up appearances instead of making progress. But you can't fake a six pack. You can't fake love. You can't fake money.

WHAT IS THE STARTING POINT FOR "HAVING IT ALL"? A willingness to face the facts. The truth. No matter how hard it is. This is the starting point for having it all. It will never come unless you are willing to tell the truth. This is the access point. There is no other way.

HOW DO YOU COME TO TERMS WITH THE REALITY OF WHERE YOU'RE AT RIGHT NOW? Stop lying. To yourself first. Then to those around you. One simple decision. Answer this: Is my life working right now...yes or no? If the answer is no, then it's time to find out why. The only way to figure that out is to quit telling stories and start telling the truth.

WHAT IS REALITY? This is a simple question. But it's not easy. So where do we start? We must be willing to look at all areas of our life. Starting with our physical reality. Is my body working for me yes or no? My nutrition? My sleep?

WHAT ABOUT MY PURPOSE? My connection with God or a higher power? Is my relationship with my wife working? Yes or No? Do my kids love me? Do they even know who I am? Am I doing what I want to be doing in life? Is my business making money?

Answering questions like these unlock the first step towards having it all.

ASSIGNMENT

1. Locate a large bathroom mirror.

2. Stand in front of it naked and stare at yourself for five minutes.

3. When your five minutes are complete, immediately right down in your workbook what you saw physically, emotionally, and spiritually.

_____
_____
_____
_____
_____
_____
_____
_____
_____
_____

4. Then record a one-minute audio in your squad chat group on what you saw in the mirror.

WEEK THREE - LIBERATION
DAY 2 TUESDAY

"We live in a fantasy world, a world of illusion. The great task in life is to find reality." - Iris Murdoch

---

FANTASY

HOLDING ONTO THE PAST

Have you ever seen the guy who still wears the same clothes he did in high school? Or the girl who styles her hair and makeup like she did when she was 18? Why do they do that? Because they can't let go of the past. They want to hold on to something they thought they had control of. And the truth is they can't.

Living in the past guarantees one thing: The same results you've been experiencing in your business. The same pain you can't seem to get rid of. The same disconnect and unhappiness you feel. Here's the crazy part: You can't change the past or control the future. But you are in charge of the NOW. The past is littered with guilt/shame, and the future is full of anxiety. The only thing you can control is what is happening right now.

It's difficult to look at what's truly going on right now. Like when I almost cut my leg off with a chain saw. That experience taught me one thing: I can't ignore reality.

It's hard to face the truth. It's ugly sometimes. There isn't anywhere to hide. But this is the only way to see what's really going on right now.

What is Insecurity?

INSECURITY: uncertainty or anxiety about oneself; lack of confidence.

The ultimate cost of caring what other people think and say? All you ever wanted. Think about it. This insecurity will keep you from saying things, doing things, or trying things you've always wanted. And it's all based on a false sense of truth.

ASSIGNMENT

Answer the following questions:

1. What is one question you refuse to answer about your life?

___

2. What are you most insecure about?

___

WEEK THREE - LIBERATION
DAY 3 WEDNESDAY

"Get your facts first. Then you can distort them as you please." - Mark Twain

---

FACTS VS FANTASY

WHAT'S THE DIFFERENCE IN LEADING WITH FEELINGS VS FACTS?

There is a reason why life seems so confusing at times. We have an issue living in real life. In the now. Instead, we've been taught to live in a fantasy. Think about it: When you were younger, your parents taught you to believe in Santa Claus and the Easter Bunny. Your life revolved around playing cops and robbers or video games depicting soldiers and outer space heroes.

And what does this lead to? A state of absolute confusion. Because we live in a space that isn't real, we attach our feelings of success and self worth to things that are not even achievable. Is Santa ever really going to get you everything you want? Are you ever going to be riding a spaceship through the cosmos? Can you just "shoot" your problems away?

WHICH LEADS US TO THE PROBLEM. Confusion and chaos. When real life doesn't act or react like our fantasies. When our wives don't lust after us like they do in the movies. When our businesses don't magically print money. When our bodies don't fit in our clothes anymore.

MEN LIE. WOMEN LIE. BUT FACTS NEVER LIE. And our inability to look at the facts as what they really are have caused this gap between what we want and what we have. And this gap is where all of our unhappiness, frustration, and anger lie.

ASSIGNMENT

Answer the following questions.

1. What fantasy are you living in today?

___

2. Inside of that fantasy who are you?

___

3. Drop a one-minute audio in your squad chat group sharing your answers.

WEEK THREE - LIBERATION
DAY 4 THURSDAY

"Our greatest weakness lies in giving up. The most certain way to succeed is always to try just one more time." - Thomas Edison

---

GIVING UP

IS THERE A PAIN OF REGRET? Looking back is not a bad thing; looking back and getting stuck is. At some point in our lives, all of us wake up and realize that the fantasy life we have been trying to live isn't working anymore. And we are unhappy with how our life has turned out. We start to look back for the moment "things went wrong". And in that process... we get stuck.

Stuck wishing things were different. Stuck wondering how things would have worked out if you hadn't been so blinded. Stuck hating what your life has become. And just like cement hardens over time, you find yourself unable to move forward from the mistakes of the past. And the longer you sit there, the more the cement hardens around you, till it feels impossible to break out.

AND WE ARE NOW UNABLE TO MOVE FORWARD. Unable to chart the course in our life that will bring us the desired results we are after. If only I had treated her better. If only I had worked out more. If only I had completed the project...then things would be different. And now, feeling stuck, we give up. Give up on the possibility that our life can ever be better. That we can ever be in love again. That we can ever build our business again with passion and purpose. That we can ever be healthy and strong again.

ASSIGNMENT

Answer the following questions:

1. Is there something in your past that you need to let go of?

2. What has this thing caused you to give up on in your life?

WEEK THREE - LIBERATION
DAY 5 FRIDAY

"The past is past and I guess if you live in the past, you cease to live." - Craig McCaw

---

BURN THE PAST

HAVE YOU EVER BEEN TO A CARNIVAL AND SEEN THE ELEPHANTS? Have you noticed how the elephant is tied up? They take them when they are still small and tie a strong rope around their necks and attach the rope to a secure pole. The baby elephants naturally try to walk away and are stopped by the rope. They pull and push and twist and turn and eventually figure out that they just aren't strong enough to break free of their shackles, so they stop resisting and just stay where they are.

The elephant becomes so accustomed to being held back by the rope, that merely the rope itself keeps the animal in check. If only they knew how powerful they really are. If only they realized that by the time they have grown up, even a rope "secured" to a pole can no longer contain them. Then they would know what true freedom is. But they don't.

SO IT IS IN OUR LIVES. We tell ourselves stories. Others tell us stories. Of how life is. How we need to act. What we need to do. They tell us our dreams and desires are fantasy. That it doesn't work like that in the real world. Until eventually, we give up. Quit trying. Quit working towards that thing we always wanted. And we find ourselves, much like the elephant, imprisoned. In our own jail cell.

AND IN OUR DESPERATION SOMETIMES, WE ASK: HOW DO I BREAK FREE? How do I bust out? Who can break the lock? We yell out, hoping someone will hear. That someone will come to our rescue. Only they don't. Why? Because they can't. They don't have the key. Only one person has the key. And that person is YOU.

You had it the whole time! You just didn't know it. So how do we actually break free? Think about this...your past is what is keeping you captive. Holding you back. Restricting your freedom. There is only one real way to break free. And that is by burning the past and unlocking your own prison door.

ASSIGNMENT

1. Identify and list out all the things that have been holding you back.

2. Find a physical representation of these. If you can't find one...write it out on a piece of paper.

3. Take a picture of these elements.

4. Find a box and put all these representations inside.

5. Once you are truly ready to let them go, find a safe place to start a fire. Bring your family with you.

6. Place your box in the fire. Watch all the labels and elements that have held you back in your past burn. As they do, feel the release and freedom you now have. Share with your family why you picked the items you did.

7. Inside your workplace group, post the picture of the things holding you back.

8. Inside your squad group, post a two-minute video talking about this experience and how it made you feel.

WEEK FOUR - DEFINITION
DAY 1 MONDAY

"It ain't what they call you, it's what you answer to." - W.C. Fields

WHO ARE YOU?

IN SCHOOL, YOU WERE ALWAYS TAUGHT TO STAY WITHIN THE LINES. The boundaries. It wasn't safe outside of them. Always ask for permission. It didn't matter if it was art class or going to the bathroom. The rules were the same. And so this pattern was instilled on you from a young age. But now, you've burnt all of those old patterns. They no longer exist. And what lies in front of you? A blank canvas.

I'm not here to tell you to believe in God or some other form of ultimate power. But I do know someone created this world that we live in, including us. Which means our ultimate happiness occurs when we are doing the same: CREATING.

THINK ABOUT IT. When you create a marriage, you're happy. When you create memories in sporting events, you're happy. When you create experiences with your kids, you're happy. When you create a business where one never existed before, you're happy. Creation brings us happiness.

AND SO IT IS WITH OUR LABELS. Our ability to create our own allows us to ultimately create our own happiness. We are always going to have labels in our lives, but instead of having ones that restrict us and cause is to want to give up, we get to create ones that build us up and inspire us to do more. It's empowering to create our own labels. Because in the end...we believe who we say we are.

ASSIGNMENT

Answer the following questions.

1. Free of all the labels that have been holding you back...who are you truly?

___

2. How does this new definition make you feel?

___

3. Drop a one-minute audio in your squad chat group sharing your answers.

WEEK FOUR - DEFINITION
DAY 2 TUESDAY

"Be who you are and say what you feel, because those who mind don't matter, and those who matter don't mind." - Bernard Baruch

THE COMPARISON OF YOU

THE OTHER DAY, I FOUND AN OLD DRIVER'S LICENSE WITH MY PICTURE ON IT. I froze for a second. Was that really me? I examined the facial features. The look in my eyes. And I shuddered. I couldn't believe it was me. I was 20 pounds heavier. I looked tired and unfocused. I had lost all motivation to do anything. When I looked at myself in the mirror, I couldn't believe I was looking at the same man.

WHAT CAUSED THIS CHANGE? How did I end up becoming the man I am today? Well, it started very simply. I defined myself. I defined who I was and who I was not. I wrote it down. I envisioned it. Thinking about it is the first step, but then we must make it a reality. There is a power of writing things down. Watching the words come alive on the page.

HOW DOES A PEN BECOME A SWORD? When the words that we wrote turn into action. Writing down who you are is not the final step. Now, armed with the game plan of the new you, action must be taken. Action based on the powerful emotions that your new reality is creating for you.

ASSIGNMENT

Answer the following questions:

1. Based on the new definition of YOU, what do you see to be the biggest difference between the new YOU and the old YOU?

2. How much more powerful does the new YOU make you feel?

WEEK FOUR - DEFINITION
DAY 3 WEDNESDAY

"The starting point of all achievement is desire." - Napoleon Hill

BELIEFS

DO YOU REMEMBER WHEN YOU WERE YOUNG, and your parents made you do chores? How much you hated it? And you would yell and scream and get in trouble. Yet, when you became a parent, you did the same thing with your kids! How do I know? Cause I did to. Any time you feel obligated to do something, you resist it. You try and find the easiest way out. There was no desire present.

IN ORDER FOR YOUR LIFE TO IMPROVE, be it with your body, your marriage, or your business, you must lay a new foundation. A new foundation based in DESIRE and not OBLIGATION. This foundation is your new belief system. Laying the foundation

WHO YOU BELIEVE YOURSELF TO BE WITH ULTIMATELY GUIDE YOUR ACTIONS. Actions based in desire. When you want to do something, then it's the first thing that gets done in a day. When you don't...you wait till the last minute. So it's important to understand that whatever you create as your new beliefs, they inspire you to take ACTION.

ASSIGNMENT

Answer the following questions.

1. With this new definition of you... what are your 3 biggest NEW beliefs?

2. How can these help lay the foundation of the new YOU?

3. Drop a one-minute audio in your squad chat group sharing your answers.

WEEK FOUR - DEFINITION
DAY 4 THURSDAY

"Don't ask the barber if you need a haircut." - Warren Buffett

LEVERAGE

WHAT IS THE DIFFERENCE BETWEEN STRENGTH AND LEVERAGE? I struggled with this for many years. I always played the "I'm alone in this world" card, therefore I don't need you to help me out. I can do it all alone. It was like trying to lift a 400-pound rock by myself. It didn't matter how strong I was, there was no way brute strength was going to move that rock.

SO HOW DO YOU MOVE THE SEEMINGLY IMPOSSIBLE? With leverage. And what is leverage? Leverage is using someone or something to maximum advantage. In the example of trying to move the rock, it would be the equivalent of using a metal pole combined with my strength to move the rock. I am leveraging the metal pole and my own strength to move the rock.

AND SO IT IS WITH LEVERAGING YOUR OWN BELIEFS. It's not just the brute strength of telling yourself you're going to increase sales by 50% or you're going to date your wife every week or you're going to lose 50 pounds. It's using those things around you, including your own strengths, to make it a reality.

ASSIGNMENT

Answer the following questions:

1. Where in your life have you leveraged who you believe yourself to be?

___

2. What were your results with that?

___

WEEK FOUR - DEFINITION
DAY 5 FRIDAY

"Personality is to a man what perfume is to a flower." - Charles Schwab

THE COLOR CODE

WE'VE TALKED THIS WEEK about defining who we are and how we can leverage those beliefs to get the results we are after in life. These beliefs create a new, more powerful version of ourselves, build on strength and possibility, not weakness and restrictions.

I SPENT MOST OF MY ADULT LIFE not really understanding what my true natural born gifts were. You see, I believed myself to be a certain way, but I didn't know how to leverage that with my gifts. So if we don't know what those gifts are, how can we leverage them to get the results we are after in life?

THESE NATURAL BORN GIFTS ARE LIKE SUPER POWERS. You must now learn how to turn on your superpowers. There is a simple way to figure out what those are. I use something called The Color Code. What is The Color Code? It is a personality test that helps you understand and leverage what your natural tendencies and gifts are. How does it work? Go to:

https://www.colorcode.com/choose_personality_test/

Choose basic (free) or full (in depth) $39.95.

ASSIGNMENT

Complete your own color code, then answer the following questions:

1. What are your strengths?

___

2. How can you leverage those strengths to build upon your new foundation?

___

3. Once you have answered these questions, record a two-minute video inside your squad chat group talking about your results.

WEEK FIVE - POSSIBILITY
DAY 1 MONDAY

"A great accomplishment shouldn't be the end of the road, just the starting point for the next leap forward." - Harvey Mackay

TARGETS

WE ARE A RESULTS DRIVEN SOCIETY. Think about it. We connect our happiness to it. More money. More sex. A nicer car. A six pack. All results. It's in our DNA. So if we are so focused on results, why do he have issues getting them?

80% OF THE POPULATION NEVER SETS TARGETS. And of the 20% that do…70% of those never hit them. Why? Because the desire for more is driven by feelings and not facts. And if you don't feel like doing it…you won't. Therefore you won't hit your target.

A GREAT WAY TO GET STARTED IS TO FOCUS ON PAST ACCOMPLISHMENTS. Past accomplishments are based on facts, not feelings. And by focusing on the facts of our past, we can see our future possibilities. Once that happens, we can then set targets into the future.

ASSIGNMENT

Answer the following questions:

1. When and where in your life have you arrived at a possibility that you saw for yourself?

2. Describe how it made you feel?

3. Drop a one-minute audio in your squad chat group sharing your answers.

WEEK FIVE - POSSIBILITY
DAY 2 TUESDAY

"Storytelling is the most powerful way to put ideas into the world today." - Robert McAfee Brown

SPEAKING BELIEF

WE TELL OURSELVES STORIES IN ORDER TO LIVE. Or at least that's what we tell ourselves. But since the dawn of society, storytelling has been a way to pass on history, traditions, and cultures. We use it to teach our kids about religion. To connect with friends and family. And to sell things in our businesses. So is storytelling a bad thing?

THERE ARE TWO DIFFERENT TYPES OF STORIES: FICTION AND NONFICTION. Fictional stories are fantasies. Like Santa Claus and the Easter Bunny. Stories that aren't really true. They are used to manipulate ourselves and others. Nonfictional stories are real. Real things that happened. Told in a way to draw us in. Connect with us.

SO WE CAN USE STORIES TO DECEIVE THOSE AROUND US, through marketing or manipulation. Or we can use them to create possibility for those around you. This is called inspiration. Inspiring people to remember things, do things, and connect with things. Getting them to take action in a positive light.

ASSIGNMENT

Answer the following questions:

1. What is one story from your life that you will tell your children about?

___

2. If you could make everyone in the world believe in one thing what would you choose?

___

WEEK FIVE - POSSIBILITY
DAY 3 WEDNESDAY

"There are two great days in a person's life - the day we were born and the day we discover why." - William Barclay

---

WHY

THE FIRST TIME I RAN A MARATHON, IT WAS A DISASTER. Literally. It was staged at a city with elevation of 6,000 feet. I had no nutrition plan. And we ran up and down a mountain. I remember getting halfway through and thinking I was ok. Then, I turned around. And it all came crashing down. I walked almost the whole way back. I wanted to quit every last step. You could say that elevation, lack of proper nutrition, or no race strategy led to my demise. I want you to consider something else: I didn't have a reason WHY. Lost in the shuffle (die at 25 and buried at 75)

I HAD NO PURPOSE. I was running just to prove to those around me that I could do it. An empty ego driven action. And that's why, when it got tough, I quit. I gave up. It was too hard. There was nothing to keep me going. There was no fuel.

CONSIDER THAT IN LIFE, THE ONE THING THAT WILL ALWAYS KEEP YOU GOING IS YOUR WHY. And what is your WHY? It's your family. Your wife. Your kids. The real reason why you work 70-80 hours in a week. The reason you want to be in shape. The reason you paint your toenails pink and build forts out of blankets.

I've done various physically strenuous events since then. A 200 mile nonstop relay race. Qualifying for the Boston Marathon (invite is based on age and time ONLY). And Warrior Week. Each of these events were extremely physically daunting. Pushing me mentally to the edge. And the only thing that got me through? My WHY.

ASSIGNMENT

Answer the following questions:

1. What is the real reason you work so hard?

___

2. Who is the one person you seek praise and admiration from in your life?

___

3. Drop a one-minute audio in your squad chat group sharing your answers.

WEEK FIVE - POSSIBILITY
DAY 4 THURSDAY

"Nothing is black-and-white, except for winning and losing, and maybe that's why people gravitate to that so much." - Steve Nash

HOW TO WIN IN LIFE

WHAT IS WINNING? According to Dictionary.com, one of the definitions of winning is "to gain the victory; overcome an adversary". Sure, it has other definitions, but this is going to be your focus. Why? Because this is the purpose in of your life. To WIN.

SO HOW HAVE YOU BEEN DEFINING WINNING? With zeroes at the end of your bank account? By the weight on the scale? By the amount of times you have sex in a week? This is how most people define it. And for most of my life, that's how I did too. But something changed when I hit rock bottom. I had to search for the reason why I was doing everything in life. And it came down to one thing.

Not too long ago, I accomplished a goal I had set for myself. To qualify for the Boston Marathon. The only way to get in was to qualify by time in my age group. I had to run at least a 3 hour and 15-minute marathon, which equals running 7:26 per mile. I trained for 6 months. I ran hard. As I got close to the finish line, winning became apparent to me. And not because I was going to hit my target (I ran 3:12). But because my 3 children were waiting to run the last ½ mile with me. That, to me, was winning.

YOU, LIKE ME, USE OTHERS TO MOTIVATE YOU TO REACH CERTAIN TARGETS. But that's all based on negativity and proving something wrong. Those people don't care about you. They will hate you before you do something and then after you accomplish it. But those who care about you will always provide the ultimate fuel for winning: LOVE.

ASSIGNMENT

Answer the following questions:

1. What does "winning in life" mean to you?

2. Who do you ultimately want to win for?

WEEK FIVE - POSSIBILITY
DAY 5 FRIDAY

"My life is like a speeding bullet that hasn't hit its target yet." - Kid Cudi

---

TRUE NORTH

WATCH THE VIDEO FIRST.

WHEN I FIRST LEARNED HOW TO SHOOT A GUN, I thought all I had to do was point my gun down range, pull the trigger, and magically hit what I was aiming for. Oddly enough, it didn't happen that way. Through proper training, I learned that I had to make sure I was aligned with the target. Through the sights. Not only seeing, it, but knowing it was arranged in a straight line.

ACTION. Knowing where you need to go is one thing. Taking the action to get there is something totally different. I won't hit the target if I never pull the trigger. The action aligned with my target makes sure I hit it. I won't be successful unless I use both.

BUT THERE IS ONE MORE THING. If my action pulls me off my target, I won't hit it either. When shooting a gun, if you pull the trigger too hard, you won't hit your target. One degree off your intended target leads to a different outcome. If you were trying to hit a target a hundred yards away, and you were just one degree off, you'd be off by 5.2 feet. Wouldn't even hit your intended target. One degree makes a huge difference.

ASSIGNMENT

1. Examine your life right now across the areas of your body, your relationship with your wife, and your business.

2. Determine what your True North looks like.

3. Write down one simple action you can take TODAY to start to move in the direction of your TRUE NORTH.

_____
_____
_____
_____
_____
_____
_____
_____

4. Now...take that action.

5. Post a two-minute video in your squad group talking about the action you took and how it made you feel after you took that action.

WEEK SIX – EMPOWERING THE MAN
DAY 1 MONDAY

"The journey of a thousand miles begins with a single step." - Tao Te Ching

P 3

WE'VE ALL BEEN IN SITUATIONS WHERE WE HAD A LONG JOURNEY AHEAD. School. Technical training. Starting a business. Training for a race. Whatever the path...it always started with one singular action. And that action, repeated consistently, allowed us to hit our target.

BUT IT WASN'T JUST THE ACTION. The action had to be in alignment with what you were trying to accomplish. Making the action smoother and easier. So what can you do to prepare? If you're preparing for a race, it's having the right shoes and hydration. If it's deploying a new product, it's having the system to support it all the way from ad to fulfillment.

THERE IS A SECRET TO GETTING WHAT YOU WANT. And that's structuring your day so that you are attacking it instead of it constantly attacking you. You put yourself in a position of advantage. And how does that start? With a simple morning routine. A morning routine helps to set the stage for better prioritizing, more effective time-management, and greater productivity throughout your day.

BY LEVERAGING YOUR TIME TO BENEFIT YOU FIRST, it allows you to hit the ground running, instead of always feeling like you're being attacked. And how do you get what you want out of life? Going after it with zeal and passion. And it all starts with your morning routine.

ASSIGNMENT

Answer the following questions:

1. What is your current morning routine?

___

2. What do you think the benefit of having one is?

___

3. Drop a one-minute audio in your squad chat group sharing your answers.

WEEK SIX – EMPOWERING THE MAN
DAY 2 TUESDAY

"The secret of your future is hidden in your daily routine." - Mike Murdock

---

P3

WHAT IS P3? P3 is a system based on years of study about human psychology and the body. About how we maximize our potential and our happiness. About how we draw close to the things and people that matter most in our lives.

THERE ARE 3 CORE AREAS WHEN WE TALK ABOUT P3. Your body, your connection with your purpose, and money. That's it. Why is it so hyper focused? Because these are the areas that generate what we want out of life. Power is derived from your Body. Purpose comes from your connection with the voice and your family. And Profit is generated as you focus on your money generating activities in life.

SO HOW DOES IT WORK? P3 works by focusing on the areas in your life that give you the daily power, clarity, and focus you need to attack the day.

POWER (BODY): Your body is the ultimate gateway to power. When you work out, your body releases endorphins, which are the natural feel good drug that it needs to get through the day. We follow that up by making the first food we take in a green drink. Why? Because it puts us in a position to make good habits when it comes to food all day long.

PURPOSE (WITH GOD AND FAMILY): Most men struggle at different points in their life wondering if they are on the right path. If they are doing what they are supposed to be doing and the way it is supposed to be done. By focusing daily on purpose through meditation, you allow yourself the course correction and inspiration needed to continue forward. Along with that, your family is your WHY.

By spending time investing with them every day, the connection, love and closeness you desire becomes a reality.

PROFIT (BUSINESS): Men are driven to provide for themselves and their loved ones. But most of the time, we just blindly go through the motions hoping things will change. A daily emphasis on how it is that you are generating income allows for you to focus on areas that need improvement or attention, thereby allowing you to become a more efficient and profitable man.

ASSIGNMENT

Answer the following questions:

1. What do you see as being your weakest area of P3?

___
___
___
___
___
___
___

2. How do you think working on that area daily will change it?

___
___
___
___
___
___
___

WEEK SIX – EMPOWERING THE MAN
DAY 3 WEDNESDAY

"An investment in self-development pays the highest dividends." - Debasish Mridha

INVESTING

THE SECRET TO SUCCESS... IS TO INVEST

When I first got married, I was told to open a savings account. I didn't understand why. I thought it was to have money for a rainy day. And it was. But what it was introducing me to, even at a very low rate, was the idea of compounding interest. As I grew older and began to actively invest my money, I saw this principle in action.

WHAT COMPOUNDING INTEREST ALLOWS YOU TO DO is make money not just on your initial monetary investment, but also on the subsequent money created by that investment. In other words, you reap rewards based on your initial actions and those actions over time.

So if we are going to receive the maximum amount of compound interest in our lives, where do you need to spend time? Think about what your greatest investment is. It's not your house, your car, or even your business. It's YOU! You are the one who created everything you have. Money, marriage, body. So ultimately, if you want more of those things, that is where your time must be spent.

FINDING THE TIME TO INVEST IS DIFFICULT FOR SOME. I get it. I was caught in that way of thinking for many years myself. I felt like I was going 100 mph from the moment I got up until the moment my head hit the pillow. I was always busy. Then my wife introduced me to something called Screen Time. It's an app for the iPhone that monitors the time you spend on it every single day. After the first week, I was floored. I had spent an average of 7 hours a day on it! That's when reality hit. I was busy being busy, but not productive. I learned that if it's important to you, then time becomes irrelevant.

ASSIGNMENT

Answer the following questions:

1. How many times a week do you invest in your body?

___

2. How many times a week do you invest in your purpose?

___

3. How many times a week do you invest in your family?

___

4. Drop a one-minute audio in your squad chat group sharing your answers.

WEEK SIX – EMPOWERING THE MAN
DAY 4 THURSDAY

"The investor of today does not profit from yesterday's growth." - Warren Buffett

PROFIT

WHAT DOES IT MEAN TO PROFIT? What is the purpose of it? For most of us, profit means to win create something more from our investment. To take something from its current state and make it better. Think about it. With money, it's making more of it. In your body, it's having a healthier and stronger version of it. In your relationship, it's having more fun, laughter and connection.

SO HOW DO YOU DEFINE PROFIT FOR YOU? Each of us is starting at a different point. And headed to a slightly different destination. But the purpose of it all is to profit. To profit from a better body, from a stronger connection, and from more money. Ultimately this is what we are after in life. More profit.

MY KIDS ARE PROBABLY MUCH LIKE YOURS. Any trip in the car that takes over 20 minutes usually includes a chorus of, "Are we there yet?" They don't want to take the time to get there, even if the destination is worth it (like Disneyland). Warren Buffett, the richest man in the world, started earning money when he was 11. He didn't see his first million until he was well into his 30's. 20 years of investment. Now? He has reaped the reward for his consistent effort, with a net worth of over $60 billion dollars.

SO HOW LONG DOES IT TAKE TO SEE THE RESULTS IN YOUR LIFE? For your body to experience change? For your marriage to light on fire? For your business to make consistent revenue? I don't have the specific answer for you. All I know is that it takes time. It has for me. But I can tell you this. It was all worth it.

ASSIGNMENT

Answer the following questions:

1. What do you see as being a win for you in your body?

   _____
   _____
   _____
   _____
   _____

2. Define a win for you in your relationship.

   _____
   _____
   _____
   _____
   _____

3. Define a win for you in your business.

   _____
   _____
   _____
   _____
   _____

WEEK SIX – EMPOWERING THE MAN
DAY 5 FRIDAY

"One of the huge imbalances in life is the disparity between your daily existence, with its routines and habits, and the dream you have within yourself of some extraordinarily satisfying way of living."
- Wayne Dyer

HOW TO IMPLEMENT P 3

WATCH THE VIDEO FIRST.

THE P3 BRINGS TOGETHER THE CORE of what is the foundation for creating the life you desire. Only through applying these daily principles will you start to see the results you've been after.

THE P3 IS BROKEN INTO 3 CATEGORIES: *Power* (Body), *Purpose* (Family/Voice), and *Profit* (Business). These three areas are the source of every man's struggles... and triumphs. By focusing on all three every single day, the game of constantly chasing after results in your body, your relationships, or your business ends. You are then able to focus on improving your overall life, and the standard of your life begins to rise.

THIS BRIEF GUIDE WAS PUT TOGETHER TO HELP YOU UNDERSTAND how to leverage this simple morning routine to obtain the results you've been so desperately seeking. By focusing on these simple actions every day, you will be able to increase the connection and achieve the outcomes you desire.

POWER (Body):

There is nowhere you will go in life without your body, so it's important that we take the time to care for the vessel that will carry us through this mortal journey.

A disciplined body leads to a disciplined mind. In other words, your body is your access point to true power. Physically, Emotionally, and Financially.

In the category of Power, we focus on two areas: *Fitness and Fuel*

Fitness: In order to unlock power, we first start by focusing on our physical activity. That's right. You can't just think about it anymore. You must move. Every day, as part of your morning routine, you must SWEAT. This can be done a number of ways. You can lift heavy. You can lift light. You can sprint. You can run far. You can do yoga.

You need to craft a routine based on your current fitness level. It can be as little as 15 minutes. What you do matters little. The important thing is that it gets done. That leads us to the next category.

Fuel: What keeps us going through the day? It's not the workout we do in the morning. It's what we feed our bodies. And what determines the food we eat? The habits we start our day with. Now, I am not a nutritionist. However, from personal experience, I know that focusing on what I put into my body has directly helped me increase strength, stamina, sleep, energy, and overall health.

So we want to keep it very basic. GET IN YOUR GREENS. That's it. How does that happen? A green smoothie. You heard me right. You aren't getting enough of the stuff that helps keep you clean and regulated. And I've learned that the easiest way to get them in is through a green smoothie. Now, what does that look like for you? It could be spinach and water. Kale and fruit. Protein and green powder. Again, the important thing is that it gets done. Make it work for you.

So, to recap, every morning we spend time focusing on powering our body. SWEAT and SMOOTHIE. That simple.

PURPOSE (Family/Voice):

The next category is PURPOSE. We focus on two areas: **Family and the Voice**.

It's interesting that the older we get, the more we want to spend time with our family. And, the more we struggle with asking ourselves if we are doing what we should be doing. Some call this a mid-life crisis.

Family: Do you ever feel out of balance? Like you spend too much time working on your business and not enough time on your family? So then you try and make it up, only to never be successful? There is a reason why. Your family is your ultimate source of energy. Think about it.

When you are fighting with your wife and angry at your kids, you can never focus on your business. No matter how hard you try. It pulls at you. It detracts you. But when you are full of love and happiness, that also bleeds over into your business. This energy pours over into your projects, marketing, and sales.

So every day, it's important that we take a few minutes to focus on our family. Your spouse and your children. How do we do this? With a simple message of appreciation, love, or honor. You can leave them sticky notes, drawings, text messages, or videos. The method doesn't matter as much as the delivery. By depositing in the family bank daily, you can then leverage that connection to help you focus on your business.

Voice: Call it praying, meditation, or whatever you want. The thing is, connection with your creator allows you to find the one thing men seek after: *Clarity*. Meditation creates space. It helps you eliminate stress. It allows you to separate all the feelings that have been causing you doubt and fear. It aligns you with your internal power.

So every day, you need to spend time connecting with your creator. It doesn't matter how you do it. There is no wrong way. Prayer, guided meditation, unguided meditation. They all serve the same purpose. Creating the space you need to make the decisions that will guide you through out life.

Now, after you meditate, it's important that you immediately write down your impressions. These are your own personal revelations. Your own guide through life. When I started writing down my impressions, I found a clarity of path that I had been missing. It allowed me to find my own answers inside instead of depending on someone else to guide me.

Your ability to focus on your connection with your family and the voice allows you to expand your mind and your heart. It fills you daily with purpose and creates the space for you to then focus all of this energy on creating one thing: Profit.

PROFIT (Business):

Money. We all want more of it. It helps us create experiences for our families. It allows us to provide for others in theirs. We bury ourselves in seminars, podcasts, audiobooks, sales funnels, and masterminds. And yet... we still don't have anything to show for it. Why? Because there is no plan. No plan for what we are going to do and how we are going to do it. So how do you overcome this? With *Strategy* and *Execution.*

Strategy: The HOW. More information won't make you money. In fact, most of it actually keeps you from doing anything at all, so it's important that we maintain that focus daily. This is accomplished through implementation to your morning routine. Now, what should you study? Again, this is all up to you. But you must be strategic about it. Where should you start? Simple. Ask yourself this question: What area of your business are you struggling with the most right now? Sales, systems, marketing, automation, fulfillment? Once you identify that area, figure out what exactly you need to learn more about. In marketing, is it sales funnel design, closing, offer creation, or something else? Now find a medium to study on. Audiobook, podcast, online course...these are all great, as long as the message is helping you solve your problem.

Execution: Now, with a clear plan, it's time to GO. What is your ACTION going to be today? The one thing that needs to get done in this area your struggling with (marketing, sales, systems, automation, fulfillment). No more talk. No more regurgitation of information. It's about the moves you're going to make to get the results you've been after. What needs to be done today to help you overcome the pain your experiencing? Make it a simple task that can be completed in one day. Is it to have a conversation with a person, hire someone, redo a sales funnel, implement a new strategy? Whatever the course of action, make sure it's related to helping you overcome your issue.

Now, this probably sounds like a lot. And it can be daunting. But I can tell you, from my own experience and the experience of thousands of men who implement a similar morning routine, this can be done. And not only that, but it will give you the clarity and daily power you need to win the daily war. The hardest battle you'll ever face... is within your own head. I promise you, that by leveraging this system, you'll gain the peace and power you will need to combat your daily battles. Time to get after it.

ASSIGNMENT

Complete the following tasks

1. Following the guide in your workbook, complete a P3 Routine.

2. Use your workbook to write down your activities.

3. Once complete, drop a two-minute video in your squad group talking about what you experienced.

- BONUS: A 30-day P3 workbook link has been emailed to you!

(NOTES)

WEEK SEVEN – LOOKING BACK TO LOOK FORWARD
DAY 1 MONDAY

"Without continual growth and progress, such words as improvement, achievement, and success have no meaning."
- Benjamin Franklin

THE FRUIT

IN ORDER FOR A FARMER TO REAP THE REWARDS OF A HARVEST, he can't just plant seeds in the ground and then disappear until harvest time. If he does that, there will be nothing to harvest. It's consistent daily action over a growing season that allows the farmer to enjoy the fruits of his labors.

WHEN MY CHILDREN WERE YOUNGER, THEY WERE OBSESSED WITH GROWING. We had a wall in our pantry where we would mark their growth every six months or so. They loved the fact that they could trace their growth. And it allowed me to appreciate it as well. And just like the farmer, these children didn't grow on their own. They needed constant nourishment, guidance, and correction.

SOCIETY IS OBSESSED WITH TRACKING TODAY. Sleep patterns, workout intensity, food consumption... but nothing when it comes to the area of defining and tracking our growth. How do you know if you are close to hitting the financial target you set for yourself months ago?

WHEN I WAS GROWING UP, WE WOULD VISIT MY GRANDMOTHER'S HOUSE REGULARLY. Every time I was there, I would run to her garden to see her grape vines. I was obsessed with their growth. From leaves, to small little spheres, and eventually to large, plump grapes. I was excited to watch the fruit progress because I knew it was getting closer to when I would be able to enjoy the fruit.

AND SO IT IS WITH YOUR LIFE. As you track and define your progress, you will be able to eventually reap the fruits of your labors.

ASSIGNMENT

Answer the following questions:

1. How do you define progress?

2. How do you track it?

3. Drop a one-minute audio in your squad chat group sharing your answers.

WEEK SEVEN – LOOKING BACK TO LOOK FORWARD
DAY 2 TUESDAY

"The ground beneath you is shifting, and either you get sucked in by holding on to old ways, or you take a giant step forward by taking some risks and seeing what happens." - Bonnie Hammer

---

LOOKING BACK

AS A KID GROWING UP, I lived away from the city with lots of open space. One of the things I loved to do was play with my sling shot. I would try to hit trees, birds, and whatever I could find. But it took me a while to figure out how a slingshot works. I couldn't just put a rock in the sling and expect it to hit something. I had to pull back, create tension, focus on what I was trying to hit, then let the momentum pull the rock forward and into the target.

DURING MY TIME AS A POLICE OFFICER, I spent a few years working on the SWAT team. One of the keys to our success was our ability to immediately dissect an operation, what went right, what went wrong, and make adjustments as necessary. But we could never make those adjustments if we weren't willing to look back and look at what truthfully happened.

HISTORY BOOKS ARE WRITTEN not only to teach us about what happened in the past, but also learn from the mistakes of those before us so that we don't make them again. Repetition of errors leads to no progress. We can't hide from our past, because if we do, it will inevitably repeat itself.

ASSIGNMENT

Answer the following questions:

1. Looking back over the last 6 months, what has been your biggest step forward?

___

2. Looking back over the last 6 months, what has been your biggest setback?

___

WEEK SEVEN – LOOKING BACK TO LOOK FORWARD
DAY 3 WEDNESDAY

"A man must be big enough to admit his mistakes, smart enough to profit from them, and strong enough to correct them."
- John Maxwell

COURSE CORRECTIONS

IMAGINE THAT IN ORDER TO WIN $1 MILLION DOLLARS all you had to do was run to an object 1 mile away. That's it. Be the first one there and win that money. What if, as you started to run, you were just one degree off the target? That's not much right? But 1 degree off will equal 92.2 feet off at one mile. 92 feet. That will guarantee you one thing: First loser.

WHY THEN, DO COURSE CORRECTIONS MATTER? Because as you get down the path heading towards your intended target, without fail, you will run into obstacles. Road blocks. People, circumstances, things that will force you to move to one way or the other. Off your direct path. Recently, my family and I visited New York City. Even though I had GPS on my phone, I got lost at least 10 times. Why? Because there was constant interference. Buildings. Subways. And it got to the point that I couldn't depend just on my phone. I needed to be able to look around at my surroundings and make adjustments as necessary.

HOW DO YOU APPLY THESE COURSE CORRECTIONS IN YOUR LIFE? You must be willing to get brutally honest with yourself. What happened? What worked? What didn't? What did I miss? What can I do better next time? The more honest you can be, then the more quickly you can course correct and get back on track to reach the prize you are after.

ASSIGNMENT

Answer the following questions:

1. What are the benefits of learning from your mistakes?

_____
_____
_____
_____
_____
_____
_____
_____

2. How important is it to quickly apply course corrections?

_____
_____
_____
_____
_____
_____
_____
_____

3. Drop a one-minute audio in your squad chat group sharing your answers.

WEEK SEVEN – LOOKING BACK TO LOOK FORWARD
DAY 4 THURSDAY

"All men can see these tactics whereby I conquer, but what none can see is the strategy out of which victory is evolved." - Sun Tzu

ALICE IN WONDERLAND

IT'S IMPORTANT TO KNOW WHERE WE ARE STARTING FROM. But it is equally as important to know where we are headed. In the famed children's book Alice in Wonderland, Alice gets lost in this new world she finds herself in. She discovers a path and begins to follow it. Soon, she gets to a tree. At the tree, the path splits left and right. She stands there, not knowing what to do. The Cheshire Cat appears in the tree. Alice asks him for help. The cat asks Alice where she wants to go. She responds, telling him she doesn't know. He then tells her, "Well then it doesn't matter which path you take."

WHEN YOU ARE UNCLEAR OF THE PATH TO WHERE YOU WANT TO GO, you become frustrated and angry. Eventually this makes you want to do one thing: Quit. But it doesn't have to be that way. Just because we get off track doesn't mean that our target has changed. It just means that our means of getting there has.

THERE IS A FALLACY THAT EXISTS IN LIFE. That multitasking is a real thing. The truth is that it doesn't. Not only can your mind only focus on one thing, but a machine works the same way. A machine is just able to do many tasks one after the other quicker and quicker. But it can't multitask. The idea that you can hit multiple targets at the same time will ultimately keep you from hitting any of them.

ASSIGNMENT

Answer the following questions:

1. Do you know where you want to go right now in your business?
   _____
   _____

2. What does that look like for you?
   _____
   _____
   _____
   _____
   _____
   _____

3. Do you know where you want to go right now in your personal life?
   _____
   _____

4. What does that look like for you?
   _____
   _____
   _____
   _____
   _____
   _____

WEEK SEVEN – LOOKING BACK TO LOOK FORWARD
DAY 5 FRIDAY

"Planning is bringing the future into the present so that you can do something about it now." - Alan Lakein

WEEKLY OPERATIONS PLAN

THE GREATEST DECISIONS MADE IN ANY TYPE OF WAR are the ones based on a man's ability to survey what is happening, course correct his energy and resources, and continue pushing forward. Every major war that has been won or lost reached that outcome not because of a decision made by a man on the front lines, but a man who was able to survey the entire battle field and make decisions based on what was happening. And so it is with your life. If you want to hit your targets consistently, then you better get damn good at being able to face reality and make adjustments when necessary.

SO HOW DOES THIS HAPPEN? How do you pull it all together? With a simple exercise I call the Weekly Operations Plan. This is where you look at the facts, strategize, course correct, and push forward towards expansion, growth and ultimately achieving the targets you are after.

YOU MEASURE, ASSESS, AND ADAPT. This allows you to compress time. Your ability to do this consistently allows you to get past the obstacles that appear quickly and efficiently. This is how you win the daily war.

ASSIGNMENT

1. WATCH THE VIDEO FIRST

2. Using the guide in the next pages of your workbook, complete a Weekly Operations Plan.

3. When you have finished the assignment, post a two-minute video in your squad group talking about what you experienced during this process.

WEEKLY OPERATIONS PLAN

 WEEKLY **OPERATIONS PLAN**

OPERATIONAL CATEGORY:

☐ SALES ☐ SYSTEMS ☐ MARKETING
☐ FULFILLMENT ☐ OTHER _____

TARGET:

_____

_____

INVOLVED PARTIES:

_____

_____

ACTION STEPS:

1. _____
   _____

2. _____
   _____

3. _____
   _____

4. _____
   _____

WEEKLY OPERATIONS PLAN

P 3

POWER:
- ☐ FITNESS
- ☐ FUEL

PURPOSE:
- ☐ VOICE
- ☐ FAMILY

PROFIT:
- ☐ STRATEGY
- ☐ EXECUTION

DAILY ACTION:

_____
_____
_____
_____
_____
_____

DAILY GRATITUDE:

_____
_____
_____
_____
_____
_____

WEEKLY **OPERATIONS PLAN**

DAILY REVELATION:

WEEKLY **OPERATIONS PLAN**

OPERATIONAL REVIEW

MISSION COMPLETE: ☐ YES   ☐ NO

WHAT WORKED:

_____
_____
_____
_____
_____
_____

WHAT DIDN'T WORK:

_____
_____
_____
_____
_____
_____
_____

WEEKLY OPERATIONS PLAN

OPERATIONAL REVIEW

WHAT DO I NEED TO COURSE CORRECT?

POWER: ☐ ON TRACK   ☐ OFF TRACK
COURSE CORRECTION

_____
_____

PURPOSE: ☐ ON TRACK   ☐ OFF TRACK
COURSE CORRECTION

_____
_____

PROFIT: ☐ ON TRACK   ☐ OFF TRACK
COURSE CORRECTION

_____
_____

DATE SELF: ☐ YES   ☐ NO
DATE SPOUSE: ☐ YES   ☐ NO
DATE KIDS: ☐ YES   ☐ NO
COURSE CORRECTION

_____
_____

WEEK EIGHT – SUCCESS CYCLE
DAY 1 MONDAY

"Hope in reality is the worst of all evils because it prolongs the torments of man." - Friedrich Nietzsche

---

EXPOSE THE DIVIDE

LET ME ASK YOU THIS A QUESTION: How much closer are you to that body you've always dreamed of? Or that marriage? That dream house? That truly successful business? Odds are...you are probably at the same place you were five or ten years ago. Why does this happen? Reality sets in. The target, although admirable, is too big for you to even comprehend how to make it happen. So you just kind of shrug, push it off to the side, and forget about it.

NEXT QUESTION: Where do you want to be in 6 months? In a year? The truth is that when you compress the timeline, it allows you to see the possibility that you want to create as being much more realistic. And the more real you think it is, the harder you are going to push to reach it.

THIS IS NOT A VISION BOARD. You're not going to talk about yachts, mansions, and traveling the world. This is real world stuff. Put all the feelings aside. Because the feelings won't get you results. You must deal in reality. With facts. Be willing to look at exactly where you are at right now. And exactly where you want to go. By a specific date. Tangible. Real.

ASSIGNMENT

1. Complete the one Expose the Divide worksheets for each of the P 3 categories on the following pages.

2. Drop a two-minute audio in your squad chat group about what you discovered during this experience.

TACTICAL BUSINESSMAN

EXPOSE THE DIVIDE

☐ **POWER** (Body) ☐ **PURPOSE** (Divine Purpose/Family) ☐ **PROFIT** (Business)

CURRENT	GAP	90 DAYS	12 MONTHS
	LEVERAGE **LEARN**		

TACTICAL BUSINESSMAN — EXPOSE THE DIVIDE

☐ **POWER** (Body)　　☐ **PURPOSE** (Divine Purpose/Family)　　☐ **PROFIT** (Business)

CURRENT	GAP	90 DAYS	12 MONTHS
	LEVERAGE		
	LEARN		

EXPOSE THE DIVIDE

☐ **POWER** (Body) ☐ **PURPOSE** (Divine Purpose/Family) ☐ **PROFIT** (Business)

CURRENT	GAP	90 DAYS	12 MONTHS
	LEVERAGE **LEARN**		

(Notes)

WEEK EIGHT – SUCCESS CYCLE
DAY 2 TUESDAY

"All who have accomplished great things have had a great aim, have fixed their gaze on a goal which was high, one which sometimes seemed impossible." - Orison Swett Marden

---

SPECIFIC AND MEASURABLE

SO HOW DO YOU DEFINE A TARGET? Have you ever been to a carnival? Tried to win the big stuffed animal for a loved one? What was the only way you actually walked away with the prize? You had to hit the target. Not almost hit it. Not graze it. But hit it dead on.

IN ORDER TO HIT ANY TARGETS IN YOUR LIFE, they must have two key characteristics: They must be specific and measurable. Why? Because if they aren't you won't ever hit them. For example, define the target of "having a better marriage". How do you hit that? What does reaching it look like? It isn't real, therefore you will never hit it.

WHEN I DISCOVERED THIS, MY WHOLE LIFE CHANGED. I understood that in order for me to actually hit something, it couldn't be a vague, blurry or unclear target. It had to be real. Tangible. Easy for me to picture. Easy for me to chase after.

ASSIGNMENT

1. In your workbook, go back to yesterday's assignment "Expose the Divide". Look at the targets you set for your 90-day cycle.

   Are they specific?

   Are they measurable?

   If not...then adjust them.

WEEK EIGHT – SUCCESS CYCLE
DAY 3 WEDNESDAY

"It is far more important to be able to hit the target than it is to haggle over who makes a weapon or who pulls a trigger."
- Dwight D Eisenhower

HITTING THE TARGET

I HAVE A FEW FRIENDS WHO ARE COMPETITION SHOOTERS. They compete in shooting events where they have a series of targets they need to hit in the least amount of time possible. The catch? They can't move on to another target until they hit the one in front of them.

THIS PRESENTS A UNIQUE APPROACH TO COMPETITION... AND LIFE. If you think about how you function on a day to day basis... is it based on working on a few different things at the same time, never actually finishing any of them? Or are you focused on finishing the one thing in front of you before you move on?

FOR MANY YEARS, I WOULD COME HOME TIRED. Telling my wife that it had been such a busy day. Then she would follow it up with, "So what did you do?" And most of the time, I struggled to find the answer. Because I had spent the day being busy, putting out fires and other small tasks. But I had really accomplished anything.

FOR A COMPETITION SHOOTER TO WIN, HE MUST HIT ALL HIS TARGETS. But he can't ever get to the last target if he never hits the first one. That's why it's so important to focus on what's in front of you right now. The one thing that needs to get done. Like a shooter who focuses with sight alignment and trigger control, so to must you focus on hitting the target in front of you if you ever want to accomplish anything worthwhile.

ASSIGNMENT

Answer the following questions:

1. What would be the benefit of focusing on one thing at a time?

___

2. Based on your 90-day target, what would be the first thing that needs to be accomplished in order for that to become a reality?

___

3. Drop a one-minute audio in your squad chat group sharing your answers.

WEEK EIGHT - SUCCESS CYCLE
DAY 4 THURSDAY

"The trouble with not having a goal is that you can spend your life running up and down the field and never score." - Bill Copeland

THE DAILY/WEEKLY GAME

LAST SUMMER, MY FAMILY AND I DECIDED TO TRY A NEW ACTIVITY. Big puzzles. My wife found a 2000-piece Star Wars themed puzzle, and we eagerly dove in. At first, it was chaos. Every kid trying to find a random piece to fit together with another random piece. Progress was slow. Frustration was high.

WE KNEW SOMETHING HAD TO CHANGE or this puzzle would never be completed. Looking at the whole picture, we started to group pieces based on color and possible relation to a character or shape. As we slowly started to work on those smaller puzzles, groups started to appear. When a few groups were put together, then we were able to add them to the larger puzzle and fit them in there. Soon, the puzzle was complete.

WHEN WE OUTLINE OUR 90 DAY SUCCESS CYCLE, it's like dumping all those chess pieces onto the table. It's a jumbled mess full of chaos and confusion. So it's important that we start to group things together and work out a strategy to eventually finish the puzzle. Working on identifying what needs to get done first, and then progressing from there, allows us to leverage the pieces themselves to achieve the outcome.

EVERYTHING YOU'VE BEEN TAUGHT SERVES A PURPOSE. It isn't random. It isn't by chance. It all has its place. The daily activity builds out the foundation. Which then allows you to work on your weekly targets. Which ultimately lead you to your 90 day success cycle outcome.

ASSIGNMENT

Answer the following questions:

1. What benefit can you see of incorporating daily and weekly activities into your 90-day success cycle?

2. Taking one of your target outcomes, what is one action you can start to take today to make it a reality?

WEEK EIGHT – SUCCESS CYCLE
DAY 5 FRIDAY

"Once you embrace the absolute truth that every leader needs a mentor, you can begin to achieve the massive growth and success that you seek." - Clay Clark

---

THE SECRET TO SUCCESS

FOR YEARS, I STRUGGLED, TRYING TO FIGURE OUT THE SECRET TO SUCCESS. Maybe it was written in scripture. Maybe in a book. Or a seminar. And no matter how hard I tried, I couldn't find it anywhere. Why? Because most people won't tell you about it. YOU have to figure it out! But I can share with you the success formula.

ALL YOU NEED IS A M.A.P. What is a M.A.P.? It involves three things: A Mentor, Accountability, and a Plan. These three things combined are what will lead you to success.

HOW DID I CREATE THIS LIFE THAT I HAVE RIGHT NOW? The wildly successful one with the passion and intimacy I always wanted? With a business full of purpose and profit? With a body full of power that I can leverage every single day? I had to use a MAP. The tens of thousands of dollars I've invested have reaped hundreds of thousands of dollars in rewards.

I FOUND A MENTOR WILLING TO HELP ME GET CLEAR ON WHAT I WANTED AND HOW TO GET IT. I leveraged a group of powerful men to get the accountability that would keep me on track. And finally, I had a clear plan of where I was going and how I was going to get there.

I CANNOT CHOOSE YOUR PATH FOR YOU. This is a path that you must define. But I can help you leverage the full power of the M.A.P.

THE MENTOR. THE ACCOUNTABILITY. THE PLAN.

ASSIGNMENT

Now you have a choice to make. Not with your head, but with your heart. It is speaking to you right now. Telling you which path to go down.

You can choose to stay where you are... or choose to chase after the life you desire.

I have 3 Options available for you:

1. If you feel drawn towards leveraging the full power of the M.A.P., then you have the option to join your fellow brothers in a small group 90 Day Success Cycle Experience.

    Go to www.thetacticalbusinessman.com/smallgroup

2. If you feel like you need specific one on one time with me to get the maximum out of your life and build a wildly successful business and personal life, then apply for One on One Training with me.

    Go to www.thetacticalbusinessman.com/oneonone

3. Or, if you feel like having access to the tools and association with the brotherhood as a whole, you can have access to me on a weekly call by leveraging option #3. Join the Academy.

    Go to www.thetacticalbusinessman.com/training

www.ingramcontent.com/pod-product-compliance
Lightning Source LLC
Chambersburg PA
CBHW080943170526
45158CB00008B/2353